Laurence Wilson

BLACKBERRY TROUT FACE

*Our society is not a community, but merely
a collection of isolated family units.*

Valerie Solanas

T0347770

OBERON BOOKS
LONDON

WWW.OBERONBOOKS.COM

First published in 2011 by Oberon Books Ltd
521 Caledonian Road, London N7 9RH
Tel: +44 (0) 20 7607 3637 / Fax: +44 (0) 20 7607 3629
e-mail: info@oberonbooks.com
www.oberonbooks.com

A catalogue record for this book is available from the British Library.

ISBN: 978-1-84943-243-6

Cover image by Andrew Tunney

For my sister, Rachel Dawn Alexandra Jones

As with all my plays they don't come together without a lot of help, advice and input from other people and *Blackberry Trout Face* went through a long process, which included contributions in different forms from the people I am now about to thank.

My better half, Amelia Stephens, for her unwavering support and advice and not to mention keeping Daisy and Poppy entertained and out of my office as I write. Daisy Wilson and Poppy Wilson, for giving me hope. Julia Samuels, Philip Osment, Keith Saha, for their dramaturgical support, belief and genius. Nicola Bentley, Tessa Buddle, David Judge, Joe Shipman, for the workshops in which they role-played up to the max. Leon Tagoe, Shaun Mason and Nicola Bently again, for script work during rehearsals for the original tour. Suzanne Bell, for turning me on to 20 Stories High and her support. 20 Stories High Youth Theatre members 2009 for sifting the dialogue for any dated words and phrases and general feedback. The Liverpool Everyman and Playhouse, for their continued support, teachings and the use of the writer's computer in the literary office. Moira Callaghan for staying at her desk so late at night at the Everyman, which meant I could work late too. Brian Way and Theatre Centre for the award. Mum for indulging my artistic side as I grew up. Dad for calling me a blackberry pudding nose almost every day of my young life, and Miss Illingworth and Mr Dixon, my old English teachers at Manor High who encouraged me to write.

Thank you all so much from the bottom of my heart.

Laurence Wilson

Characters

JAKEY – Age 18.
White. He is big and strong for his age.

KERRIE – Age 15.
Mixed-race. Tough, almost a tomboy.

CAMERON – Age 13.
Mixed-race. Small and thin.

KERRIE, JAKEY and CAMERON
have the same mother but different fathers.

SCENE 1 – FREE GIFT

Early October. Tuesday morning. The kitchen of an Edwardian terrace house somewhere in Liverpool. It is the only occupied building in a street that has otherwise been vacated and tinned up. The kitchen is fairly big and is cluttered, with everything from dirty and clean washing, pots and pans, McDonalds free toys, a few books, and bills.

Nothing matches, including the chairs and table and a shoddy, two seat sofa. There are two worktops in an L-shape. The smaller having an almost finished construction of a model bridge on it, with the rest of the pieces and tools scattered around it. On the other worktop are coffee, tea and sugar tins and a bright yellow sharps bin.

JAKEY enters; he has the air of an angry dog about him and a number one haircut with a big scar visible on one side. He wears the street clothing of a local youth gang member, black tracksuit and black trainers. He has hold of a letter, which he puts on the worktop and opens the fridge and takes out a carton of milk, sniffs it and deciding it's okay, has a swig. He picks the letter back up, opens it quickly and reads it. He smiles. CAMERON enters, he is wearing his school uniform, which is very crumpled and out of shape, one arm slightly longer than the other, with silvery snot trails on the sleeves. He is thin and timid looking, and a bit twitchy; he is carrying a Transformer toy. JAKEY immediately stuffs the letter in his pocket.

CAMERON: What was that?

JAKEY: What was what?

CAMERON: What yer just stuffed in yer pocket?

JAKEY: Nothin.

CAMERON: Yer not in trouble again are yer?

JAKEY: It's a letter off me ex.

CAMERON: She wrote yer a letter?

JAKEY: She wants me back.

CAMERON: She didn't just text yer?

JAKEY: No.

CAMERON: Or facebook yer?

JAKEY: No.

CAMERON: That's just weird. Can I see it?

JAKEY: Did you sleep in them last night? *(Indicates CAMERON's school uniform.)*

CAMERON: Yeah.

JAKEY: Why?

CAMERON: It's what's it, innit?

JAKEY: What?

CAMERON: Economical.

JAKEY: Is it?

CAMERON: What's the point of takin it off to go to bed, when the first thing yer do when yer wake up, is put it straight back on again?

JAKEY: You'll have to get changed into yer spare.

CAMERON: Why?

JAKEY: I can't have me little brother walkin around like some tramp.

CAMERON: I haven't got a spare.

JAKEY: She's only got yer the one uniform?

CAMERON: This used to be yours.

JAKEY: Lad, I was never that skinny.

CAMERON: That's why Kerrie boiled it in a pan for us.

JAKEY: Did what?

CAMERON: To shrink it.

JAKEY: Unreal.

CAMERON puts his Transformer down and gets up and takes some silver foil from the draw and grabs an old plastic toy helmet from the floor. He then sits down and starts covering the helmet in the silver foil.

CAMERON: Why are yer up?

JAKEY: Coz I am.

CAMERON: But yer never usually get up until about half one.

JAKEY: Call the bizzies!!!

CAMERON: Are yer goin somewhere?

JAKEY looks at CAMERON and then looks as if he's going to say something, as KERRIE enters. KERRIE is in a rush and has the air of a busy bee. She has her school uniform on, it is neat and tidy. She hardly glances at the boys and heads over to a drawer by the sharps bin. She opens the drawer and looks puzzled. She tries the drawer next to it. She turns around to look at her brothers.

KERRIE: What have yer done with it?

JAKEY: Done with what?

KERRIE: Don't play games.

CAMERON: What's up?

KERRIE: As if yer don't know.

CAMERON: I don't, honest.

KERRIE: Don't do this to her.

CAMERON: Isn't her stuff there?

KERRIE: This isn't fair. Yers haven't got any idea of the pain, have yer?

JAKEY: Shut up.

KERRIE: Just give it to me.

JAKEY: I haven't got it.

KERRIE: Tell me where it is then.

JAKEY: She must of got it.

KERRIE: I take it up every mornin.

JAKEY: Cameron, have you hid it?

CAMERON: No. I don't like it when she hasn't got any.

KERRIE takes this in and then rushes back out.

KERRIE: *(O.S.)(Shouts.)* Mum!

CAMERON: Have yer hid it?

JAKEY: I'm not interested.

KERRIE: *(V.O.)* Mum!!

JAKEY: Mouth on that.

KERRIE: *(V.O.)* Mum!!!

CAMERON: Why isn't she answerin?

After a few more moments KERRIE comes charging back in.

KERRIE: She's not here.

JAKEY: I heard the door go at about five this mornin.

KERRIE: Where would she be goin at that time?

CAMERON: Pass us the Frosties Kerrie.

JAKEY: Make sure yer save me some lad.

KERRIE: Something's wrong.

CAMERON: Frosties!

KERRIE grabs a box of Frosties off the worktop and passes them to CAMERON, who is still covering the hat.

KERRIE: Where would she go?

CAMERON: Bowls.

KERRIE: What?

CAMERON: Bowls and milk.

KERRIE gets the bowls and milk and goes and looks out the window.

KERRIE: Did she go out the front or back?

JAKEY: Front. *(Beat.)* Sounded like she was draggin somethin heavy.

CAMERON: Like a body???

JAKEY: Sounded more like a big bag or somethin.

KERRIE: But where would she be goin with a big bag at five o'clock in the mornin?

Short pause.

CAMERON: Hurry up with them will yer.

KERRIE: What?

KERRIE looks at the milk and the bowls in her hands and then gives them to CAMERON.

KERRIE: Why didn't yer get up and see where she was goin?

JAKEY: Because I don't care where she's goin.

KERRIE: Well yer should care.

JAKEY: Why?

KERRIE: Because she's yer Mum.

JAKEY: She's nothin.

CAMERON: Maybe she went the launderette.

KERRIE: At five in the mornin?

JAKEY: Sounded like she got in a car.

KERRIE: A car?

JAKEY: Yeah.

KERRIE is shocked by this. She exits. CAMERON finishes covering the hat and then puts it on.

JAKEY: What's that?

CAMERON: I'm making an invisibility suit. This bit's the helmet.

JAKEY: Invisibility suit?

CAMERON: The silver foil will bend the light around me, if I angle it just right and then no one will be able to see me.

JAKEY: Yer thirteen now lad, not three.

CAMERON: It's on the back of this old comic. *(Holds up an old comic from the 1960s.)* How to make yer own invisibility suit.

JAKEY: It won't work.

CAMERON: We'll see.

KERRIE comes back into the room.

KERRIE: All her clothes are gone.

JAKEY: She must of been draggin a suitcase then.

CAMERON: When it's all done, I'll be able to wear it to the shops.

JAKEY: Yer better not even think of goin outside with that on.

CAMERON: *(Realizing a flaw in his plans.)* But then they wouldn't be able to see me to serve me.

CAMERON pours his Frosties into his bowl. An envelope falls out.

CAMERON: Yes!

KERRIE: What?

CAMERON: Looks like I've won somethin.

KERRIE: Oh.

JAKEY: Nice one. What have we won?

CAMERON: It might be a ticket to Willy Wonka's Chocolate Factory.

JAKEY: Get a grip.

CAMERON picks up the letter and reads the front.

CAMERON: It's for you Jakey.

JAKEY: Me?

JAKEY takes the letter. KERRIE is anxious. JAKEY opens it and reads it.

CAMERON: What does it say?

JAKEY gives it to KERRIE.

CAMERON: Read it out Kerrie.

KERRIE reads it to herself. Her face becomes a mixture of shock, confusion and fear.

CAMERON: What does it say?

KERRIE: She can't do this.

JAKEY: She's done it.

KERRIE: She can't.

CAMERON: What's she done?

KERRIE: She needs me.

CAMERON: What does it say?

KERRIE: It must be a joke.

JAKEY: Nah.

KERRIE: She's playin a trick on us.

CAMERON: What trick?

KERRIE: She wouldn't do this to me.

CAMERON: Do what?

JAKEY: She's run away.

KERRIE: No.

CAMERON: Why would she run away?

KERRIE: It doesn't say that.

JAKEY: As good as.

KERRIE: It's a trick.

CAMERON: Let me see.

KERRIE gives it to CAMERON.

CAMERON: Just says she's goin away for a while.

KERRIE: *(To the ceiling.)* Very funny Mum.

CAMERON: Where's she gone?

JAKEY: Does it say where?

CAMERON: No.

JAKEY: There yer are then.

CAMERON: Oh. *(Beat.)* But when's she coming back?

JAKEY: Does it say when?

CAMERON: No.

JAKEY: There yer are then.

> *Silence. CAMERON absorbs what the letter means as KERRIE sits down.*

CAMERON: She's run away.

KERRIE: It doesn't say that.

JAKEY: Doesn't have to. Even bonehead's on to it.

CAMERON: I'm not a bonehead. *(Beat.)* Who's goin to walk me to school? *(Beat.)* She says she's left some money under the microwave.

> *CAMERON goes over to the microwave and grabs the hidden money from underneath.*

CAMERON: 50 quid.

JAKEY: Is that it?

CAMERON: And a piece of newspaper cuttin.

KERRIE: About what?

CAMERON: It's an advert for a job.

JAKEY: Bring it here.

> *CAMERON brings it over and gives it to JAKEY.*

JAKEY: For Netto. *(Beat.)* What's that all about?

CAMERON: *(Beat.)* It's obvious. Yer need to get a job.

JAKEY: What?

CAMERON: If Mum's gone, yer need to get work. Me and Kerrie are too young.

JAKEY: What do I need to get a job for?

CAMERON: So yer can buy food and that.

JAKEY: Jokin aren't yer.

KERRIE: Cameron, she's not gonna be away long enough for £50 to run out.

KERRIE pulls her mobile phone out of her pocket and taps the buttons.

JAKEY: Let me get this right, she thinks she can just do a runner and I'll take over? Think again.

CAMERON: Somebody's got to look after us!

KERRIE: Her phone's switched off.

She starts texting.

KERRIE: I can't believe she's done this. I thought we was getting somewhere. She was gettin ready to go into rehab.

JAKEY: Yer've got more chance of Cammy shittin gold bricks, than her goin into rehab.

KERRIE: Shut up.

CAMERON: How are we gonna eat?

JAKEY: I don't need no money to eat lad. I've got me skills.

CAMERON: What skills?

KERRIE sends her text.

JAKEY: Survival skills. I can live off the land me.

CAMERON: How?

JAKEY: Me Dad taught me to.

CAMERON: What does he know?

JAKEY: He was a traveller wasn't he.

CAMERON: Yeah but if yer get a job we can get Sky Plus.

JAKEY's face says it all.

KERRIE: We need to try and understand what's happened here?

JAKEY: What's to understand?

KERRIE: She wouldn't just go without tellin me.

JAKEY: She only cares about herself.

KERRIE: That's not true.

JAKEY: What kind of a mother would let their own kid get up every morning and do her fix for her?

KERRIE: I don't do her fix for her I just get her stuff ready. Anyway, she's been actin weird for weeks now. Not goin out.

JAKEY: I haven't got time for any of this. I'm outta here.

CAMERON: *(Panicked.)* Where yer goin Jakey?

JAKEY: Campin.

KERRIE: Typical.

CAMERON: Yer can't.

JAKEY: There's money there, Kerrie'll look after yer.

CAMERON: Don't leave me Jakey.

JAKEY: It's just for a few days lad.

CAMERON: They'll beat me.

JAKEY: Kerrie's here.

CAMERON: They're not scared of Kerrie.

KERRIE: I wouldn't stick up for yer if they were.

CAMERON: Why not?

KERRIE: Coz yer a selfish little maggot.

CAMERON: I'm not.

KERRIE: Mum's gone, and all you care about is how yer gonna eat and who's gonna walk yer to school.

JAKEY: I'm off.

CAMERON: I won't let yer. *(Blocks exit.)*

JAKEY: *(Laughs.)* Move it.

CAMERON: I won't.

JAKEY: *(Pulls him out of his way.)* Move.

CAMERON: Please Jakey, please...

CAMERON starts having a panic attack.

JAKEY: I don't believe this.

CAMERON: I can't breathe...

KERRIE: Just take a deep breath.

CAMERON: Can't... Can't breathe...

KERRIE: Remember what the doctor told yer to do.

CAMERON takes deep breaths.

JAKEY: He's puttin it on.

KERRIE: What would you know about it?

JAKEY: I'm gone.

KERRIE: She's left you in charge.

JAKEY: I have to go.

KERRIE: Why?

JAKEY: I have to prepare meself.

KERRIE: For what?

JAKEY: *(Beat.)* Go and stay with Auntie Carol.

KERRIE: She won't have nothin to do with us no more.

JAKEY: Yeah, because skag face robbed all her jewellery.

KERRIE: Don't call her that.

JAKEY: No one in the family will have nothin to do with us because of that bag head.

KERRIE: Don't call her names. She's a heroin addict. It's an illness. *(Beat.)* We haven't got no one else to look after us Jakey.

JAKEY: I'll be back in three days.

JAKEY grabs a backpack and a fishing rod.

CAMERON: Jakey?

JAKEY leaves through the back door. CAMERON rushes after him.

CAMERON: Don't go Jakey. What am I gonna do?

KERRIE: Go to school.

CAMERON: I can't.

KERRIE: Move it.

CAMERON: But Mum takes me.

KERRIE: Tough.

CAMERON: I can't go on me own.

KERRIE: It's all your fault she's gone. Playin up all the time. So get yer arse down to that school now or I'll slap yer meself.

CAMERON: Will you walk me there?

KERRIE: I'm gonna look for Mum.

CAMERON: Please.

KERRIE: I need to find her.

CAMERON: Don't make me go on me own.

KERRIE is confused.

CAMERON: Please Kerrie.

KERRIE: Go and get me coat, it's on me bed.

CAMERON heads off upstairs. KERRIE goes over to her mother's letter and picks it up; she holds it to her chest and starts to cry.

End of scene.

SCENE 2 – PRODIGAL SLUM

Three days later. Late afternoon.

KERRIE is stood at the worktop, working on her model bridge. There is a noise from the hall. KERRIE turns round.

KERRIE: Mum?

The door from the hallway opens and CAMERON staggers in. He has a black eye and his nose is bleeding.

CAMERON: Where were yer Kerrie?

KERRIE: I was lookin for Mum.

CAMERON: Yer promised yer'd come and walk me home again.

KERRIE: What happened to yer?

CAMERON: What's it look like?

KERRIE: Are yer hurt?

CAMERON: Doesn't look like yer lookin for Mum to me.

KERRIE: I've only been back a few minutes. Workin on this helps me think.

CAMERON puts his hand on his head and winces.

KERRIE: What's up?

CAMERON: They hit me over the head with somethin.

KERRIE: What?

CAMERON: I don't know everythin went all weird for a bit.

KERRIE: I better take yer to hozzy.

CAMERON: No, no way.

KERRIE: Yer might be concussed.

CAMERON: They'll start askin questions. They'll wanna know where Mum is. They'll put me into a home and I'm not goin back there.

KERRIE: I'm doin me best here Cameron. None of this is my fault. And I tell yer something else lad; if yer keep up this bad attitude I'll drag yer down to that care home and throw yer through the window.

CAMERON runs out the kitchen and upstairs.

KERRIE: *(Shouting after him.)* Go on lock yerself in yer room yer little prick. *(Beat.)* Cam… Cam I'm sorry…just come down and I'll try and sort yer head out.

There is no answer. KERRIE shrugs and goes back to her model.

JAKEY enters from the back door carrying his rod, backpack and something wrapped up in newspaper. He is swaggering and puffing with pride.

JAKEY: Now then, the hunter has returned.

He throws the newspaper wrap on to the kitchen table with a thud.

JAKEY: Take it she hasn't come back?

KERRIE looks at him and then back at her construction.

JAKEY: Has she phoned?

KERRIE: No.

JAKEY: Texted?

KERRIE ignores him. JAKEY puts the rod and pack down in a corner.

JAKEY: Yer should of seen me out there girl, I was like Rambo or somethin.

KERRIE continues to work on the model.

JAKEY: Proper livin off the fat of the land. Couple of perch on me first night, even dug up a few carrots and spuds from a farm to go with it.

KERRIE drops a piece of model.

KERRIE: Shit!

JAKEY: Roasted it on a spit.

KERRIE fishes out a new one.

JAKEY: De-e-licious.

KERRIE turns round.

KERRIE: Oh well isn't that great. I'm over the moon for yer. Because, while you've been playin Tarzan the Ape Head, we've been livin on brown sauce crackers.

She picks up a half-eaten cracker with brown sauce spread on it.

JAKEY: Didn't yer buy no food with that fifty quid?

KERRIE: One of Mum's dealers knocked round after yer left and said she owed him ninety.

JAKEY: What did yer let him in for?

KERRIE: I was lonely.

JAKEY shakes his head.

KERRIE: And the fact he was wavin a monkey wrench in me face, had somethin to do with it an all. I mean call me old-fashioned Jakey but I've always thought I had the wrong shaped face to wear a monkey wrench buried in me forehead.

JAKEY: I'd have smacked his head in.

KERRIE: If yer weren't out bein some plazzy Rambo yer mean?

JAKEY: I was in tune with nature.

KERRIE: Trippin on mushies more like. *(Beat.)* Yer should be out there lookin for her.

JAKEY: Is that what you've been doin?

KERRIE: I've been everywhere. Over and over. No one's seen her. No one knows nothing. I can only look for her durin school time coz Cameron throws a fit if I try and go out when he's home. Has she phoned you?

JAKEY: She hasn't got me number.

Pause.

JAKEY: Has anyone else been round?

KERRIE: No.

JAKEY: Are yer sure?

KERRIE: Hang on, I nearly forgot, Robert Patterson knocked round and asked me if I wanted a back rub and a pedicure but I turned him down, because I was too busy tryin to swallow brown sauce crackers.

JAKEY: *(Beat.)* I've got somethin for yer here.

JAKEY picks up the newspaper wrap.

KERRIE: Why do yer keep comin in the back way?

JAKEY: Lost me keys. Get on this.

JAKEY slaps the newspaper wrap down next to KERRIE's model.

KERRIE: What?

JAKEY: Open it.

KERRIE: It stinks.

JAKEY: That's the smell of life that girl. *(Beat.)* Come on, open it.

She unravels the paper to reveal two big, fresh trout. KERRIE wrinkles her nose.

JAKEY: Trout, fresh from the Alt this mornin.

KERRIE: Yer expect me to eat this?

JAKEY: Better than brown sauce crackers.

KERRIE: Why did yer leave us on our own?

JAKEY: I'm back now aren't I?

KERRIE: Somebody crack open the champagne; Jakey's back.

JAKEY: Everythin's alright innit?

KERRIE: Our Mum's run away, and we don't know were she is, or what state she's in, or nothin. We've got no food, no money and no one to look after us. Apart from that everythins proper hunky funky like.

JAKEY: You've got food now.

KERRIE: But we haven't got no one to look after us.

JAKEY: I'm back for now aren't I?

KERRIE: For now?

JAKEY: Just chillax.

Short pause.

KERRIE: What if she's in trouble Jakey?

JAKEY: She's not.

KERRIE: How do you know?

JAKEY: Coz if she was in trouble she'd involve us.

KERRIE: I don't know what to do.

JAKEY: Get these cooked for a start.

KERRIE: What, yer think I'm gonna do all the cookin coz I'm female?

JAKEY: Well yer do anyway don't yer?

KERRIE: Pourin hot water on to a few pot noodles isn't exactly cookin Jakey.

JAKEY: Bang them in the microwave.

KERRIE: They've got eyes.

JAKEY: That's so they don't bump into other fishes.

KERRIE grabs the fish and then places them on a plate from the rack, bangs them into the microwave and switches it on. She then goes back over to her model and carries on working on it.

JAKEY: What is that anyway?

KERRIE: What does it look like?

JAKEY: The Runcorn Bridge.

KERRIE: There's yer answer then.

JAKEY: What do yer wanna make a model of the Runcorn Bridge for?

KERRIE: Because it's a great piece of engineerin.

JAKEY: It's proper ugly more like.

KERRIE: It's beautiful. A compression arch suspended-deck bridge.

720,000 rivets.

JAKEY: Boring.

KERRIE: It's a special place.

JAKEY: What's the big deal with bridges anyway?

KERRIE: Bridges bring everythin together.

JAKEY thinks about what KERRIE has said.

KERRIE: Have yer got anythin else besides the fish?

JAKEY: No.

KERRIE: *(Beat.)* Take Cam to the bit of waste ground at the back of the entry?

JAKEY: What for?

KERRIE: There's loads of brambles down there.

JAKEY: I'm not followin yer.

KERRIE: Last time I looked they was full of big blackberries.

JAKEY: Yer want me to take him blackberry pickin?

KERRIE: We used to do it with Nan. Look, it'll be somethin else to eat.

JAKEY: He does me head in.

KERRIE: He wouldn't be a proper little brother if he didn't.

JAKEY: Anyway it's freezin out there now. Gonna be a bad night.

KERRIE: Is that what Rambo'd say? I was gonna go and shoot some Russians but I forgot to bring me thermal undies.

JAKEY: I've got better things to do with me time.

KERRIE: What like hang around the streets with yer gang, makin everyone cross the road?

JAKEY: I caught the fish, so you can go blackberry pickin. Where is the little ball bag anyway?

KERRIE: Locked himself in his room again.

JAKEY: What for?

KERRIE: I forgot to walk him home and he got beat up.

JAKEY: Yer wha? Who by?

KERRIE: I dunno.

JAKEY: I've had enough of all this. The lad needs to step up.

JAKEY heads for the hall.

KERRIE: What are yer gonna do?

JAKEY: *(O.S.)* Cam, get yer arse down here now. *(Beat.)* Cameron, if yer don't get down here now I'm gonna come up there, break yer door down and smash all yer toys up.

CAMERON comes down the stairs.

JAKEY: *(O.S.)* Get in there.

CAMERON enters the kitchen followed by JAKEY.

JAKEY: What happened?

CAMERON: Tazer and his mates jumped me outside the school gates.

JAKEY: I thought they didn't pick on yer no more.

CAMERON: They didn't.

JAKEY looks troubled.

CAMERON: They were sayin things about Mum.

KERRIE: What were they sayin?

JAKEY sits down.

CAMERON: I don't know. I couldn't hear properly because me ears went all funny when I got hit in the head. I said I'd get you on to them Jakey. But they just laughed at me.

JAKEY: Did yer fight back?

CAMERON: They're gonna pay for it now aren't they Jakey?

JAKEY: Did yer give as good as yer got?

CAMERON: Wait til they see you Jakey.

JAKEY: *(Louder.)* Did yer have a go?

CAMERON: Yer know I can't fight.

JAKEY: It's not about what yer can do; it's about havin a go.

CAMERON: I don't want to hurt no one.

JAKEY: But it's alright for me to go round smackin heads for yer, is that it? I'm gonna teach you how to look after yerself lad.

CAMERON: I don't need to look after meself, I've got you.

JAKEY: Where's the respect in that?

CAMERON doesn't answer.

JAKEY: Where's me gloves?

JAKEY searches the kitchen.

KERRIE: Don't be stupid Jakey; he's been hit enough for one day.

JAKEY: He can't go through life relyin on his big bro to keep bailin him out.

JAKEY grabs his boxing kit from the corner of the room, two sets of gloves and some pads. He discards the pads and throws a pair of gloves at CAMERON.

JAKEY: Put them on then.

CAMERON: I don't want to.

JAKEY: I said, put them on!

CAMERON reluctantly starts putting the gloves on as JAKEY puts on his.

KERRIE: Look at him. He's not built like you.

JAKEY: That's coz his dad's a maggot.

CAMERON: He's not.

JAKEY: I say he is. What are yer gonna do about it?

CAMERON just stands there.

JAKEY: Come on, son of a maggot.

CAMERON doesn't move.

JAKEY: Come on.

CAMERON shakes his head.

JAKEY: Come here.

CAMERON skulks over.

JAKEY: Let's see what yer've got.

CAMERON: I haven't got anythin.

JAKEY: Hit me.

CAMERON: I don't want to hit yer.

JAKEY: Just do it.

CAMERON: No.

JAKEY: Come on, I can take it.

KERRIE: Do it some other time Jakey.

JAKEY: Just take a swing at me will yer?

CAMERON: No.

JAKEY: Come on yer chicken.

JAKEY punches CAMERON just hard enough to hurt a little.

CAMERON: Ow!

KERRIE: Jakey!

JAKEY: Put yer guard up.

CAMERON doesn't and JAKEY takes a slightly harder swing at him and connects.

KERRIE: Stop it.

KERRIE grabs JAKEY's arm to try and stop him but he pushes her over.

JAKEY: Stay out of it! Come on yer little ball bag, let's see what yer've got.

CAMERON: I haven't got nothin.

KERRIE: That's enough.

JAKEY: Shut up! Fight me!

JAKEY takes another swing at CAMERON. This one is hard enough to make him stagger.

JAKEY: Come on yer little prick!

KERRIE: You've hurt him.

JAKEY: I'll smack his head in if he doesn't fight back.

JAKEY takes another swing at CAMERON and this time he knocks him to the floor.

CAMERON: I'm sorry, I'm sorry, I'm sorry…

CAMERON starts hyperventilating, his breath coming in and out in short, ragged stabs. JAKEY stands over him appalled at his brother's weakness.

KERRIE: Look what yer've done now. He's havin another panic attack.

JAKEY: Old women have panic attacks.

KERRIE helps CAMERON sit up.

KERRIE: Just try and breathe slowly.

CAMERON: Can't...

KERRIE: He's not gonna hit yer again.

CAMERON: I can't breath, can't breath, can't...

KERRIE gently strokes CAMERON's cheeks and hair and whispers in his ear and he starts to calm down a bit.

KERRIE: Nice and slow.

JAKEY: Yer gonna have to learn to fight back.

CAMERON gets up.

CAMERON: I won't.

He runs out of the room into the hall and up the stairs.

KERRIE: Get off on that did yer?

JAKEY: I'm tryin to help him.

KERRIE: Goin blackberry pickin would of helped him Jakey.

JAKEY heads for the doorway into the hall.

KERRIE: Where are yer goin?

JAKEY: To talk to him.

KERRIE: Don't yer think yer've done enough?

JAKEY stops. KERRIE brushes past him out of the room.

KERRIE: Yer wouldn't even know what to say to him because yer never here for any of this.

KERRIE leaves. JAKEY stands there looking at the door. A few moments pass and JAKEY's phone rings. He takes it out of his pocket and looks at the caller name. He lets it ring out and then puts it back in his pocket. He is left with just the whirring of the microwave, which suddenly dings. JAKEY looks over at it and then goes over and opens the door. Smoke pours out. His phone starts ringing again. He grabs a pair of hair straighteners from the worktop and uses them to pull out the trout. They have been well overcooked, shrivelled to less than a quarter of their original size and are now rock hard. JAKEY stands there looking at them; they seem to be a symbol of his failure to provide.

End of scene.

SCENE 3 – CAM AND JERRIE

The next morning at 3am. The kitchen.

It is dark but a dull light above the stove gives the room some illumination. A strong wind howls outside. The oven is switched on and the door is open. KERRIE and CAMERON are lying under a patchwork quilt on the sofa. They are asleep. JAKEY appears through the doorway from the yard, carrying two heavy looking plastic bags. He puts them on the worktop. He notices KERRIE and CAMERON and then spots a sweatshirt and pants that have silver foil stuck all over them and he picks them up and looks at them. He shakes his head, guessing it must be the rest of CAMERON's invisibility suit. He puts it down and then crouches down by the oven; warming his hands. KERRIE's mobile phone is on the table and it suddenly springs to life. It's the Psycho Shower Scene tone and it blasts out at full blast. JAKEY near jumps out of his skin and KERRIE and CAMERON sit up.

JAKEY: Shit!

KERRIE gets up and rushes over to the phone and picks it up.

CAMERON: Is it Mum?

The phone goes again in her hands and this time KERRIE jumps.

CAMERON: Is it, Kerrie?

KERRIE: Must be.

It goes again. She opens the messages.

KERRIE: Me messages have got through.

KERRIE calls her Mum as her brothers watch and wait.

KERRIE: She's not answerin.

JAKEY: There's a surprise.

KERRIE tries again.

JAKEY: What are yers doin down here anyway?

CAMERON: The gas has gone off.

JAKEY: It hasn't has it?

CAMERON: Yeah, it was proper dead cold upstairs, so we come down here about midnight and put the oven on to keep warm.

JAKEY: Yer wanna be out in it lad.

JAKEY turns the main light on.

CAMERON: Where've yer been.

JAKEY: Doin me bit.

CAMERON: What do yer mean?

JAKEY: Providin.

JAKEY smiles and grabs a washing basket with clean clothes in and empties it on to the floor.

KERRIE: It's cut off now. Her battery must of run out or somethin. *(Notices washing.)* What are yer doin, it's clean all that?

JAKEY puts the empty basket on the table and then picks up the plastic bags he brought in and puts them down next to it. KERRIE and CAMERON look at each other and then back at JAKEY expectantly. JAKEY takes one of the bags and tips it over the basket and several pounds of blackberries pour out into it.

JAKEY: Blackberries!

KERRIE: *(Withering.)* Wow.

JAKEY: Yer don't sound too happy there girl.

CAMERON: What's in the other bag?

JAKEY: Have a look.

CAMERON and KERRIE both peer inside the other bag.

CAMERON: Rabbits?

JAKEY: Ten out of ten for observation lad.

CAMERON: Did yer trap them?

JAKEY: Caught them with me bear hands lad.

CAMERON: Wow. You're Rambo.

JAKEY: Tellin yer.

KERRIE: They've got floppy ears.

JAKEY: So would you if yer'd just been throttled.

KERRIE: No, they've got floppy ears, as in, they're floppy eared rabbits.

CAMERON: Are they easier to catch?

KERRIE: They're pets.

CAMERON: Pets?

KERRIE: Yer don't get wild floppy eared rabbits. He's been in someone's rabbit hutch for them.

CAMERON: Have yer?

JAKEY: Would I do that?

KERRIE: I bet they're from that big house on the other side of the back field.

CAMERON: The one Nan said she was gonna buy us if she won the lottery?

KERRIE: Yeah, they've got rabbits.

JAKEY: They'll fill yer belly won't they.

KERRIE: Have you been smokin glue?

JAKEY: Yer don't smoke glue yer sniff it.

KERRIE: Well yer must of been sniffin it then, if you think I'm gonna eat some kid's floppy eared bunny rabbits.

JAKEY: You're proper ungrateful you.

KERRIE: Ungrateful?

JAKEY: Yeah.

KERRIE: Yer think yer the big provider because yer come in here with a couple of dead pets and a bag of blackberries.

JAKEY: You told me to pick them.

KERRIE: With Cammy.

JAKEY: He was asleep. Anyway I nearly froze me bollocks off out there pickin these. It's the coldest September in an hundred years yer know.

KERRIE: What do yer want me to do about it?

JAKEY: Eat them.

KERRIE: You eat them.

JAKEY: No, you eat them.

KERRIE: No, you eat them.

JAKEY: No, you eat them

JAKEY grabs a big handful of blackberries from the basket.

KERRIE: No, you eat them.

CAMERON: I'll eat them.

JAKEY: Ladies first.

JAKEY comes closer to KERRIE.

KERRIE: What, yer think I'm gonna eat them out of your hand?

JAKEY: Too right yer are.

JAKEY squashes the blackberries into KERRIE's face.

KERRIE: Arrh!!! What are yer doin???

JAKEY and CAMERON laugh. KERRIE grabs a handful of blackberries and shoves them into JAKEY's face.

JAKEY: Oh, you're gettin it now.

JAKEY grabs another handful of blackberries and chases KERRIE around the table.

KERRIE: Get away.

JAKEY: Cut her off Cam.

CAMERON makes a move.

KERRIE: You dare.

CAMERON stops.

JAKEY: Get her.

KERRIE: Get him.

CAMERON doesn't know which way to turn. JAKEY stops and focuses on his little brother.

JAKEY: Sittin on the fence eh? The punishment is death by blackberries. Get him.

CAMERON: No!

KERRIE and JAKEY grab CAMERON and push his head into the basket of ripe purple fruit.

CAMERON: Arh, it's freezin!

They dunk him in and out a few times and then they suddenly all burst out laughing, CAMERON joins in.

JAKEY: We better get this washed off before it stains us purple.

CAMERON: *(Monster voice.)* I'm a Purple People Eater.

KERRIE: Purple what?

CAMERON: People Eater... It's a game. Me Dad got me it from a car boot sale.

KERRIE: Never heard of it.

CAMERON: Do yers wanna play it?

KERRIE: Let's get washed first.

JAKEY is about to fill the washbowl.

JAKEY: The water'll be freezing.

KERRIE: Boil the kettle.

JAKEY switches the kettle on and it starts to heat up.

JAKEY: Soon as we're washed, I'll get skinning them rabbits.

KERRIE: I've told yer I'm not eatin...

The electric cuts off, extinguishing the oven, the light and the kettle. JAKEY notices the kettle die down.

JAKEY: The leccy's gone off.

KERRIE: Arh, no way.

JAKEY: Put the emergency credit on.

CAMERON: That was the emergency credit.

KERRIE heads over to the drawers.

JAKEY: Are yer sure?

CAMERON: I think so.

JAKEY: Go and check.

KERRIE pulls out two cheap battery operated lamps and places them on the table. She pushes them and they light up.

KERRIE: I'll go.

KERRIE goes out into the hall, heading for the front door.

JAKEY checks the kettle.

JAKEY: It's warm enough. *(Beat.)* You're gonna have to get over all this crap lad. Yer've just gotta get out there and yer'll see it isn't as bad as yer think it is.

CAMERON: Nobody likes me. They wanna hurt me.

JAKEY pours the warm water into the bowl and puts a sponge in.

JAKEY: People round here, they smell fear, the way animals can; it gets them all thingioed... nervy or somethin... Uncomfy.

CAMERON: I don't mean to.

JAKEY: I mean yer won't even go the shop on yer own.

JAKEY starts washing CAMERON.

JAKEY: It's all in yer head anyway lad. Yer wanna start growin up and stop playin with toys and all that. Throw them Transformers away. *(Beat.)* Yer Dad doesn't help, getting yer them. My Dad never bought me no toys ever.

CAMERON: That's sad.

JAKEY: No it's not lad. Coz what he done was taught me how to survive. Do yer know what he did for me tenth birthday?

CAMERON: No.

JAKEY: He took me to a forest in the middle of nowhere and left me there. Said I had to sleep the night there on me own and then find me own way home.

CAMERON: What did he do that for?

JAKEY: Rights of passage wannit. Do yer know what he got me for me fourteenth?

CAMERON: No.

JAKEY: This. *(He pulls out a knife from his pants.)* He said, when he was my age, they used to settle any disputes with their fists. But now it's all knives, and he said if I didn't move with the times then I was goin down.

CAMERON: I don't like your Dad Jakey. He put my Dad in hospital and now he won't come here no more.

JAKEY: Yer can find him easy enough lad. Sellin the Big Issue on Bold Street. *(Beat.)* If your Dad was more like mine, yer wouldn't be afraid to go out would yer?

CAMERON: Maybe not Jakey but at least I'm not afraid of me Dad.

JAKEY pauses for a moment. CAMERON is pretty much clean, so JAKEY washes himself. KERRIE enters rubbing her hands together briskly.

KERRIE: The leccy hatch was frozen shut. I had to knock it open with a brick.

JAKEY: No emergency credit?

KERRIE: No.

JAKEY: Let's get yer cleaned before the water goes cold.

KERRIE goes over to the bowl and JAKEY takes the sponge and washes his sister.

JAKEY: If we was caught out in the wild like this, yer know what we'd do?

KERRIE: We're not in the wild.

JAKEY: We'd dig up a load of moss and fern leaves and pile it into like a big thingio...er blanket and get under it.

Water drips down KERRIE's neck.

KERRIE: Watch it, it's all drippin down the back of me neck.

JAKEY: Come on let's go all Siberian and get under this quilt.

They go over to the couch, which is a two seater and squeeze in on it. They pull the patchwork quilt over themselves.

JAKEY: I was there when Nan first started makin this.

KERRIE: Took her about three years to finish it.

JAKEY: She took her time like.

KERRIE: It's because she had arthritis in her fingers. I used to rub cream on them and paint her nails.

JAKEY: *(Beat.)* See this one. *(Points to a patch.)* She cut that from your first babygrow Cam.

CAMERON: Did she?

JAKEY: Yeah, that's yours, that's Kerrie's and this one's mine.

They start scrutinizing the patches.

JAKEY: Look at that.

CAMERON: What is it?

JAKEY: Pikachu. I forgot... Yeah she er...she took it off me favourite t-shirt because I wouldn't stop wearin it. That's why he's so faded. I think I only give it up because she promised to sew it into this.

KERRIE: Oh my God, that's a bit of me bridesmaid dress from when Auntie Carol got married.

CAMERON: That's Nan's old curtains.

KERRIE: Jakey!

JAKEY: I'm not snugglin.

KERRIE: You so are snugglin.

CAMERON: *(Beat.)* Why didn't Mum go to her funeral?

JAKEY: Coz she was too smacked up.

KERRIE: That's not true.

CAMERON: Why didn't she then?

KERRIE: Coz she was too heartbroken.

JAKEY: They hated each other.

KERRIE: If Mum hated her so much then why did she take an overdose after her funeral.

Short pause.

CAMERON: Do yous believe in heaven?

JAKEY: Nah, I reckon yer just turn into nothin. Life is like a big spliff and the roach is death.

KERRIE: I believe in heaven.

CAMERON: Is that where Nan is then?

KERRIE: Course.

CAMERON: Do yer think she's watchin us now?

JAKEY: No, coz I reckon her idea of heaven, will be watchin back to back episodes of Columbo.

KERRIE: God, she used to make us watch that with her.

JAKEY: With a mug of pink milk.

CAMERON: I used to fall asleep on her knee.

KERRIE: Jakey.

JAKEY: What?

KERRIE: I never thanked yer.

JAKEY: What for?

KERRIE: For savin Mum. I mean, everythin went so fast and we just...we just got caught up in it all, and before we knew, them social workers was cartin us off to them homes. *(Beat.)* Yer brought her back to life all on yer own and yer was only a kid. You was so brave Jakey. Yer didn't give up. Yer kept breathin into her mouth and pushin her chest and it seemed like forever but yer kept on and yer done it. Yer brought her back. *(Beat.)* And I know it really touched her that, when I told her what yer'd done. She went clean for nearly six weeks.

JAKEY: Still wasn't enough though was it?

Pause.

CAMERON: Is that an Action Man outfit?

KERRIE and JAKEY look at it and then at each other.

KERRIE: *(Pointing to another patch.)* Yeah and that's me Barbie doll dress.

CAMERON: Why did she put them in?

KERRIE: Nan said this quilt was gonna be like a fingio... Arh... What are they called?... A tapestry. Me and Jakey was always playing with Action Man and Barbie weren't we Jakey. *(Beat.)* We had our own little world... It was called Jerrie.

CAMERON: Jerrie?

KERRIE: It's our two names mixed together.

CAMERON: Oh, yeah.

KERRIE: A magical island.

CAMERON: Wow.

KERRIE: Jakey's Action Man and my Barbie were the stars of it.

CAMERON: I thought yer said yer had no toys.

JAKEY: Shut up.

KERRIE: He so did. He used to hide them in a shoebox, when his Dad come round.

JAKEY: I never.

KERRIE: First of all, Barbie and Action Man was washed up on opposite sides of the island and they had to fight their way through all these scary monsters and deadly beasts to get to this like er...little oasis in the middle, where nothin bad would happen.

CAMERON: Yeah?

KERRIE: And that's where they met and fell in love. They even got married.

KERRIE: We made a pact when we was in Jerrie.

CAMERON: What kind of pact?

KERRIE: Tell him Jakey.

JAKEY: I can't remember no pact.

KERRIE: I can. *(Beat.)* Item (1.) Never ever take heroin. Item (2.) Never ever, ever leave each other. Item (3.) Never ever, ever, ever have baked beans without cheese on top.

CAMERON smiles. KERRIE and JAKEY are lost in the past for a moment. CAMERON thinks about what's been revealed.

CAMERON: What happened to Jerrie?

KERRIE: *(Meaning JAKEY.)* He grew up; started knockin round the streets with the gang.

JAKEY: You started bein her skivvy more like. Stuck to her like a fly on shit.

CAMERON: Yer mean Mum?

KERRIE: I had to look after her. Make sure she didn't...

CAMERON: Didn't what?

KERRIE: She needs support.

JAKEY: It's time you got real.

KERRIE: Like you yer mean?

JAKEY: Yeah.

KERRIE: If you're so real then how come yer hidin here?

JAKEY: Yer what?

KERRIE: Comin in and out the back way. Goin campin on yer own. Ignorin yer phone. Yer haven't been hangin out with yer gang for weeks now. So come on Jakey be real and tell us what's goin on.

JAKEY: I'm er... Nothin... It's just... It's time to move on that's all.

CAMERON: Move on to what Jakey?

JAKEY: Just move on.

KERRIE: Are you in some sort of trouble or somethin?

JAKEY: No. *(Beat.)* Anyway it's time you moved on.

KERRIE: Oh yeah?

JAKEY: I mean haven't yer got no ambitions?

KERRIE: Yeah, to get Mum clean.

JAKEY: That's not an ambition that's a life sentence.

KERRIE: I was gettin close. We was talking about it; makin plans.

JAKEY: Who are yer heroes Kerrie? Who do yer wanna be like?

KERRIE: Edgar Cardoso, James Buchanan Eads, Isambard Kingdom/ Brunel

JAKEY: / Never heard of any of them.

CAMERON: I bet they all made bridges.

KERRIE: Yeah, they're the best.

JAKEY: Okay, so yer wanna make bridges. So why don't yer?

KERRIE: I've got me hands full here.

JAKEY: Not anymore.

KERRIE: She'll be back soon, I know she will. I think she's gone to a clinic.

JAKEY: Then why wouldn't she of just said so? Why would she have made out she's run away?

KERRIE: I don't know. She's not been herself for the last couple of weeks.

JAKEY: How do yer mean?

CAMERON: She come home one night and she was shakin really bad?

JAKEY: Rattlin?

CAMERON: More like somethin really bad had happened to her.

KERRIE: We couldn't get nothin out of her but after that she stopped goin out. That dealer who took the money started bringin her stuff here.

CAMERON: She had a nosebleed an all.

JAKEY: When was this?

KERRIE: About two weeks ago.

JAKEY looks troubled. He is wrestling with something.

JAKEY: Do yer ever wonder where she goes?

KERRIE: What, when she goes out?

JAKEY: Yeah.

Suddenly KERRIE's phone goes again. This time it's the Dexter's Laboratory theme tune. They all jump again.

KERRIE: It's a message.

She jumps up and rushes over to the table, picks up the phone and smiles from ear to ear.

KERRIE: It's her.

CAMERON jumps up.

CAMERON: What does she say?

KERRIE opens the message.

KERRIE: *(Reading.)* I love you all.

CAMERON: Is that it?

KERRIE: She loves us.

CAMERON: Doesn't it say she's on her way back?

KERRIE: She loves us, so she must be coming back?

CAMERON: When?

KERRIE: She'll be on her way now. She got me messages and now she's on her way back and yer know what else?

CAMERON: What?

KERRIE: She'll be clean.

CAMERON: Will she Jakey?

JAKEY doesn't answer and instead stands up and goes over to the back window. KERRIE starts texting back.

KERRIE: I knew she wouldn't let us down Cam. We're gonna be a happy family again.

JAKEY: Get under the quilt.

They all snuggle up under the patchwork.

JAKEY: Get on this.

JAKEY plays a track on his mobile phone, it is 'Us and Them' by Pink Floyd. Time passes and the three of them fall asleep. More time passes. KERRIE's mobile suddenly bursts into life, it's another message. She still has it in her hand and silences it almost immediately. Her brothers stir but do not wake. She looks at it and smiles and then opens the message. Her eyes widen; she seems to think for a moment, as though the phone has asked her a question or offered up a puzzle. Then she seems to get the answer as her face turns into an even bigger smile. She looks at her brothers and then deciding not to wake them, she gets out from under the quilt, slips into her UGG Boots, grabs her coat and takes a piece of paper from the drawer and writes something on it and puts it on the table. Having done that she leaves, using the front door. Her brothers continue to sleep soundly.

End of scene.

SCENE 4 – ALL THE DIRTY PLACES

Same day. About seven hours later. The kitchen. We can hear rain lashing down outside. CAMERON comes in panting from the hallway, he has his brother's coat on and is soaking wet.

JAKEY: *(From the hall.)* Kerrie? Kerrie?

JAKEY enters looking around, dripping with rainwater.

JAKEY: She here?

CAMERON: Dunno.

CAMERON: Why can't we find her?

JAKEY: We will.

CAMERON gazes into nowhere.

CAMERON: Why didn't she wake us up? We all could have gone to meet Mum.

JAKEY shrugs and looks round for a dry top.

CAMERON: Do yer think she's really is with Mum?

JAKEY: *(Picking the note up off the table.)* It's what she wrote innit?

CAMERON: Am I doin good Jakey?

JAKEY: Yer doin great. I wouldn't know where to look without yer.

CAMERON: I keep thinking someone's gonna grab me.

JAKEY: But yer still out there with me. Yer showin some guts at last lad.

JAKEY pats CAMERON and then rushes out and upstairs.

CAMERON's hands have been stuffed in the pockets of JAKEY's coat all this time. He now takes them out so that he can take it off. Something in one of the pockets, caught by his hand, pops out and falls to the floor. CAMERON picks it up. It is the letter that JAKEY hid from him. CAMERON looks at it. He walks to the door and listens for JAKEY. He then opens it and reads. His face drops. He shakes his head and his breathing becomes laboured. He is fighting back a panic attack. JAKEY comes back in in new clothes and holding CAMERON's coat.

JAKEY: Right, shift yer… What's up with you?

CAMERON doesn't answer.

JAKEY: Come on, I need me little sidekick. *(Beat.)* Cam.

CAMERON: What's the point?

JAKEY: Cam?

CAM doesn't answer.

JAKEY: Get your arse out there now!

CAMERON: I won't.

JAKEY: Don't be messin with me lad, I need your help out there now!

CAM sits on the sofa.

JAKEY: Get up!

CAMERON: I will if yer promise.

JAKEY: Promise what?

CAMERON: You'll always stay and look after me.

JAKEY grabs CAMERON.

JAKEY: What's the matter with you eh? Why can't yer just be normal?

CAMERON just stares at JAKEY.

JAKEY: You embarrass me.

CAMERON just looks through JAKEY.

JAKEY: Yer sister's out there right now and anything could be happenin to her but you wanna hide here like some rat. Don't yer care what happens to her?

CAMERON: You never have. You've never cared about any of us!

JAKEY: Yer think I should care about a snotrag like you?

JAKEY pushes CAMERON backwards and he crashes into KERRIE's model bridge. The delicate structure breaks and bends out of shape.

JAKEY: Look what yer've gone and done now.

CAMERON: *(Beat.)* Are you leavin us?

62

JAKEY: What are yer on about?

CAMERON: Nothin.

CAMERON starts picking up the bridge. JAKEY throws CAMERON's coat at him.

JAKEY: Never mind that. Get that on and...

KERRIE enters. She is absolutely drenched. She looks totally dejected.

JAKEY: Kerrie.

She ignores her brothers and walks over to her damaged model bridge and looks at it.

JAKEY: Where've yer been, I've been worried sick about yer?

KERRIE doesn't answer.

JAKEY: Yer should of told us where you were going.

KERRIE doesn't respond.

JAKEY: I thought somethin had happened to yer. *(Beat.)* We've been lookin everywhere. *(Beat.)* No one had seen yer.

KERRIE touches the bridge.

JAKEY: Where was yer?

KERRIE doesn't answer.

CAMERON: Did yer find her?

JAKEY: Look at the state of yer.

CAMERON: Where is she?

JAKEY: Did somebody hurt yer?

No response.

CAMERON: Is she comin back?

JAKEY: I'll kill them if they did.

KERRIE looks at JAKEY.

JAKEY: What's up with yer?

KERRIE: Don't yer even want to know if I met her?

CAMERON: Did yer?

KERRIE: She sent me a text. It said, I'm at a special place. So I thought I knew where she was. There's this park right near the river, where yer can see the Runcorn Bridge. I've been there with me Mum a few times. We'd sit off and look at it and I'd tell her all the stuff I knew about it, while we had a flask of tea and some cookies. We called it our special place. *(Beat.)* So I thought she had to be there.

It was freezin but I didn't care coz I knew she was gonna be there, waitin for me. I kept thinkin, she'll hug away the cold.

JAKEY: Yer should of woke us up.

KERRIE: It was still dark when I got there. The bridge was all lit up though and it was all reflectin in the water and it looked dead beautiful.

JAKEY: Yer need to get out of these clothes, before yer get sick.

KERRIE: She wasn't there. So I texted her and I waited.

JAKEY: Get her a towel Cam.

CAMERON starts searching the washing for a towel.

KERRIE: I waited for a reply.

JAKEY: Take yer coat off.

JAKEY unbuttons KERRIE's coat.

KERRIE: But the special place she was at, wasn't our special place.

JAKEY pulls her coat off.

KERRIE: I kept textin her and textin her, telling her where I was; to come and get me, until I had none left. Then the sun come up and the bridge wasn't beautiful anymore. Just a bridge. Ugly, cold metal. *(Beat.)* Then finally she texted me back.

JAKEY: Where's that towel?

CAMERON finds a towel and takes it over.

CAMERON: What did it say?

KERRIE: She said she's with some old friends from years ago, on the South Coast and that they're overlookin some river. She said there's this really nice little bridge goin across it and that it reminds her of me. A special place. She said she'll tell me about it one day when she sees me. Oh yeah and er... Keep safe.

CAMERON looks at JAKEY and then holds out the towel for KERRIE. She doesn't take it. JAKEY takes the towel from CAMERON and starts drying KERRIE's hair with it.

CAMERON: What are yer doin Jakey?

JAKEY: What does it look like?

CAMERON: Looks like yer pretendin to care about Kerrie.

JAKEY: I don't want her to get sick do I?

CAMERON: No, coz that wouldn't look good when they come and drag us off to the care home would it.

KERRIE: Care home?

CAMERON: Is this gonna be our rites of passage Jakey. Leavin us in a home like yer Dad left you in a forest.

KERRIE: What are yer on about?

CAMERON: This.

CAMERON pulls the letter from his pocket. JAKEY stops rubbing KERRIE's hair.

JAKEY: What's that?

CAMERON: I just found it in your pocket.

JAKEY: Give it here.

KERRIE: What's goin on?

CAMERON: Tell her Jakey.

KERRIE: What?

JAKEY: *(Beat.)* I'm joining the army. *(Beat.)* In five days.

KERRIE: Is this a joke?

JAKEY: No.

JAKEY lets go of the towel and it drops to the floor. He moves away from KERRIE.

KERRIE: How can yer even think about goin at a time like this?

JAKEY: I just/ can…

KERRIE: What about us?

JAKEY: Yer see, I had all of this planned before she run away.

CAMERON: What have we done?

JAKEY: No…it's…it's not about you…

CAMERON: I can try and change Jakey. Maybe you'll like me if I can change.

JAKEY: I just…I just have to get away from here.

KERRIE: Why?

JAKEY: It's her fault. She's done this.

KERRIE: Mum?

JAKEY: Look, we can spend the next five days together and then I'll have to go.

KERRIE: What will yer do? Drop us off at the care home or do we have to make our own way?

JAKEY: It's not my fault.

CAMERON: You have to stay and look after us.

JAKEY: Yer not my kids, it's not my problem.

KERRIE: Why's it Mum's fault?

JAKEY: Somethin happened.

KERRIE: Like what?

JAKEY: A couple of weeks ago.

KERRIE: What happened?

JAKEY: Yer don't wanna know about this.

JAKEY: Just forget about it?

KERRIE: Tell me.

JAKEY: We was out an about see. I was just like er...sittin off on a wall and a few of the little dickheads started happy slappin some prozzy. They was pushin her round and she come near enough for me to see her properly. *(Beat.)* It was her.

CAMERON: Who?

JAKEY: Mum.

KERRIE and CAMERON are taken aback.

JAKEY: Her nose was bleedin and she was dead scared, shakin...and she...she looked so...so small... She was... she was beggin them to stop.

KERRIE: Mum.

JAKEY: She saw me and I thought she'd...but she...she didn't... She didn't say me name... She... She didn't want them to know she knew me... She didn't...didn't want them to know that she was...that she was me Mum.

KERRIE: God...

JAKEY: None of them hadn't never seen me with her, so they didn't know who she was. They started eggin me to hit her. I grabbed hold of her. She was just...just lookin at me... She made me feel sick. I wanted to...wanted to smash her face in.

KERRIE: Jakey...

JAKEY: They was all shoutin, smack that bitch Jakey, smack that bitch. So I pulled me fist back. I wanted to hit her. I could see me knuckles smashin into her nose, I saw meself just hittin her and hittin her over and over until she had no face left. They was all like, what are yer waitin for Jakey? Smack the bitch. And then it just came out.

CAMERON: What did?

JAKEY: I said, this bitch is my Mum. They all started laughin. So I repeated it. This bitch is my Mum. They got it that time. She started cryin and everyone just stood there. I looked at her and I looked at them. If it had been anyone else they'd been slappin around, I'd have done nothing. Coz that's what it is out there.

Then I told her to go and she did. I watched her walk off all funny coz one of her heels had broke off. No one said nothin but I knew that was it for me. I don't want none of it no more. I've gotta go, and the army is me only way out.

KERRIE and CAMERON take a moment to absorb this.

CAMERON: Yer can just stay here with us.

JAKEY: Yer think yer can just leave a gang like that and walk round like yer was never a part of it? Yer think they'll have that? The things I know, the things I've seen. It doesn't work like that. It's lifetime membership. The only way to escape is to disappear, one way or the other. I've just had enough of it. I hate it. I've gotta get away from them.

CAMERON: We can go somewhere else.

JAKEY: I'm sorry Kerrie. I didn't tell yer. I didn't want yer to know what Mum does when she goes out.

KERRIE: What? Yer think I don't know what she does?

JAKEY: Yer knew she was…

KERRIE: A prozzy? Street walker? Sex worker?

JAKEY: How long's she…?

KERRIE: About six months.

JAKEY: Why?

KERRIE: They stopped her benefits.

JAKEY: She should have said.

KERRIE: Why what would yer have done Jakey? Gone out and got a job instead of leachin off her? What she was doin, was keeping this roof over your head and putting food in yer belly.

JAKEY: Yer can't blame all this on me.

KERRIE: She's all I had and now she's gone because of you. You've been makin her feel like she was nothing for years now and then yer nearly smash her face in, because she was doin the only thing she could to keep us safe. That must have been that night she come back in pieces. You've driven her out. Yer should of told me what happened so I could of helped her.

JAKEY: What difference would it have made? You've never helped her ever. Alls you've ever done is make it easier for her to be what she is.

KERRIE: You should of gone then. Instead of hidin. She would have stayed then. And now you're goin and leavin us with nothin.

JAKEY: Every day out there with them I'm... I'm becomin... Losin it... Another couple of months on, I might have done it. I might of joined in. Because she'd just be another victim like all the rest. *(Beat.)* I have to go.

CAMERON: What about me?

JAKEY: *(Beat.)* I can't help yer no more lad.

CAMERON: They've already started beatin me again.

JAKEY: I'm joinin the army.

CAMERON: Yer can't do that.

JAKEY: It's what I want.

CAMERON: No!

JAKEY: It's somethin I've been thinking about for a while. What happened with Mum just pushed me to do somethin about it. *(Beat.)* I'm sorry.

CAMERON: No!!!

CAMERON suddenly slaps JAKEY hard across the face. JAKEY takes it. CAMERON slaps him again and again JAKEY takes it. CAMERON picks one of the kitchen chairs and waves it menacingly at his older brother. JAKEY doesn't move. KERRIE watches.

CAMERON: Come on fight me.

KERRIE: Put it down Cameron.

CAMERON: He has to stay and teach me how to fight.

KERRIE: Put it down.

CAMERON: Yer said yer'd teach me Jakey. I'm ready now.

KERRIE: Cam.

CAMERON: I'll make yer proud of me.

KERRIE: Let him go.

CAMERON: Why won't he fight me?

KERRIE: Because he's a coward. And he can't keep his word.

JAKEY: I never gave me word.

KERRIE: Item (2.) Never ever, ever, leave each other.

JAKEY: That's just stupid kids stuff.

KERRIE grabs JAKEY's tent pack and rod and takes them over to him. She holds them out for him to take.

KERRIE: We don't want yer here.

CAMERON: We do.

JAKEY: I've got five days.

KERRIE: Spend them somewhere else.

CAMERON: No don't.

KERRIE: We don't need yer Jakey.

JAKEY tries to find something to say but can't find the words. He picks up his things and leaves.

CAMERON: Jakey! I'm sorry. I'm sorry.

KERRIE: You wouldn't care if that was me would yer?

CAMERON: I would.

KERRIE: Nah, all you care about is protection. If that was me who'd gone and he'd stayed yer wouldn't care.

CAMERON: It's not true.

KERRIE: So yer think I'm gonna look after yer now?

CAMERON: I know yer will.

KERRIE: Yer don't know nothin.

CAMERON: Yer not like him.

KERRIE: I'm a mug yer mean?

CAMERON: No.

KERRIE: A stupid, skivvy, pushover doormat?

CAMERON: No.

KERRIE: Because I'm through.

CAMERON: I'll help out. Do yer want me to fix yer bridge?

CAMERON starts frantically picking pieces of the bridge up and tries to fix it. As he does this, KERRIE takes a small paper wrap out of her pocket. She goes over to the drawer she first opened at the beginning and pulls out a needle, a spoon, some vinegar, a longish piece of rubber hosing and a lighter. She takes it all over to the table. CAMERON sees what she's doing.

CAMERON: What are yer doin?

She opens the wrap and then pours out the brown powdery contents on to the spoon.

CAMERON: Where did yer get that from?

KERRIE: I know all the dirty, nasty little places.

CAMERON: What?

KERRIE heats up the spoon with a lighter.

CAMERON: Stop it!

KERRIE: I'll be able to understand her now.

CAMERON: I'm gonna get Jakey.

CAMERON starts putting on his invisibility suit.

KERRIE: You can't go out there.

CAMERON: I can.

KERRIE: Yer really think that's gonna make you invisible? Yer gonna get yer head smashed in.

CAMERON: Just wait...just...just wait a minute.

CAMERON puts on his invisibility suit and runs out of the kitchen and out of the house.

She now adds the vinegar to the heroin. Having done that she starts using the lighter to warm it up. The heated vinegar dissolves the powder. KERRIE then draws the liquid up into the syringe and sits down on the couch, and rests the needle on the arm rest. KERRIE then takes off her sodden pyjama top (she is wearing a vest underneath) and then starts using the rubber hosing as a tourniquet on her left arm. She pulls it tight and taps at a bulging vein. She takes a deep breath and brings the needle over it, ready to puncture the skin. Just then JAKEY bursts in followed by CAMERON.

JAKEY: Yer worth more than that.

KERRIE: I'm not worth nothin.

JAKEY: No, that's not true.

KERRIE: Mum doesn't want me and you don't want me, even Cammy doesn't want me.

JAKEY: I do. That's why I've come back.

KERRIE: Only because Cam went and got yer.

JAKEY: *(Beat.)* Cam, there's a box on top of me wardrobe. Will yer go and get it for me?

CAMERON: Yeah.

CAMERON rushes out.

KERRIE: I gave up everythin for her.

JAKEY: I know yer did.

KERRIE: What's the point?

JAKEY: Cameron needs yer. *(Beat.)* I need yer.

KERRIE: I thought she needed me but it was all lies. I thought I knew everythin about her but I knew nothin. And that's what I am Jakey, nothin. But this. *(Indicates needle.)* This will make me somethin.

CAMERON enters with a shoebox and holds it out to JAKEY, who doesn't take it but instead takes the lid off and puts his hand inside and suddenly pulls up an old battered Action Man with no legs, closely followed by a Barbie Doll in a wedding dress.

JAKEY: See. I kept them all these years.

KERRIE: *(Beat.)* They're dead Jakey.

CAMERON grabs the ACTION MAN and wiggles it at KERRIE.

CAMERON: *(ACTION MAN.)* Hi Kerrie!

KERRIE looks at him.

CAMERON: *(ACTION MAN.)* Don't suppose you've seen Barbie anywhere have yer?

KERRIE looks at JAKEY, who pulls a face.

CAMERON: Hey Barbie there you are. I've been lookin all over Jerrie for you.

JAKEY looks uncomfortable.

CAMERON: What's up toots? Cat got yer tongue?

KERRIE looks at JAKEY expectantly. CAMERON gives him a not-so-subtle nod.

CAMERON: *(ACTION MAN.)* I said has the cat got your tongue?

JAKEY: *(Usual voice.)* No. *(BARBIE.)* I mean er…no.

KERRIE stifles a laugh.

CAMERON: *(ACTION MAN.)* Good. Now listen up Barb.

JAKEY: *(BARBIE.)* I'm all ears.

CAMERON: *(ACTION MAN.)* Well actually from where I'm standing you're all fake boobies.

JAKEY: *(BARBIE.)* I'll have you know that they are 100% real.

KERRIE laughs.

CAMERON: *(ACTION MAN.)* Anyway, I'm off the point here. I just want you to know that losing my legs kinda messed me up for a while there but I'm off the booze, I've stopped sniffing paint stripper and I want us to get back together. What do you say Barb.

KERRIE picks up CAMERON's Transformer.

JAKEY: *(BARBIE.)* Well I do need to wash my hair/ and

KERRIE wiggles the Transformer.

KERRIE: *(TRANSFORMER.)* Wait up doll face. You sure you wanna get back with that slack ass?

CAMERON: *(ACTION MAN.)* Say what?

KERRIE: *(TRANSFORMER.)* I mean I'm back on the market since Darth Vader blasted my girlfriend, Robin Reliant into a black hole.

CAMERON: Darth Vader's from Star Wars not Transformers.

KERRIE: I'm mixin it up. *(TRANSFORMER.)* So do you want to be my gal?

JAKEY: *(BARBIE.)* No but you can turn into a car and give me a lift to the hairdressers.

KERRIE starts to cry and laugh all jumbled together. Her emotions are all over the place. JAKEY and CAMERON laugh with her and are also quite emotional but not crying. As the laughter starts to die down, KERRIE picks up the needle and JAKEY and CAMERON stop. She takes it over to the sharps bin and drops it in it.

JAKEY: We need to renew our vows.

KERRIE: OK. Item (1.) Never ever take heroin.

JAKEY/CAMERON: Item (1.) Never ever take heroin.

KERRIE: Item (2.) Never ever, ever, leave each other.

JAKEY/CAMERON: Item (2.) Never ever, ever, leave each other.

KERRIE: Item (3.) Never ever, ever, ever have baked beans without cheese on top.

JAKEY/CAMERON: Item (3.) Never ever, ever, ever have baked beans without cheese on top.

CAMERON: Can I add a new one?

KERRIE: Course yer can.

CAMERON: Item (4.) Always try to be ourselves.

JAKEY/KERRIE: Item (4.) Always try to be ourselves.

End of scene.

SCENE 5 – THE ONE THAT'S GOT TO STAY

Two weeks later. The kitchen. Teatime.

CAMERON is mopping the floor. KERRIE is setting the table.

She is now wearing an apron. There are four places. KERRIE drops some cutlery on the floor.

CAMERON: What's the matter with you?

KERRIE: I don't know I'm just dead nervous.

CAMERON: She's not comin for another half hour.

KERRIE: I know I just want everythin to be right for her.

CAMERON: It will be. I mean look at this floor for a start. She'll be able to eat her dinner off it.

KERRIE: I think we'll stick to the table.

CAMERON: So what are we havin?

KERRIE: Sautéed Rainbow Trout with Green Tomato and Blackberry Sauce.

CAMERON: How did yer put that together?

KERRIE pulls out a Nintendo DS from her apron and opens the screen. It was on standby, so comes on immediately.

CAMERON: You've got a DS?

KERRIE: I borrowed it off Latoya Dean.

CAMERON: How's that helpin yer cook.

KERRIE selects something on the screen.

KERRIE: Come Here.

CAMERON looks at the screen.

KERRIE: Sauteed Rainbow Trout with Green Tomato and Blackberry Sauce. There's all the ingredients and what to do and that.

KERRIE closes it.

CAMERON: You've got a DS and yer usin it to cook?

KERRIE: Too right I am.

CAMERON: Aren't there no games with it?

KERRIE: I didn't lend no games.

CAMERON: That's just stupid.

KERRIE: Yer won't be sayin that when yer droolin over yer dinner.

JAKEY enters from the front way. He is dressed in a security uniform.

JAKEY: What! Somethin smells proper good.

KERRIE: Do yer think?

JAKEY: Tellin yer, I could smell it down the street.

KERRIE: Did yer get the apple pie?

JAKEY: Here.

JAKEY hands the bag to KERRIE.

CAMERON: Catch any robbers?

JAKEY goes to frown but something gets the better of him, and the frown becomes a warm smile.

KERRIE looks in the bag.

KERRIE: Where's the custard?

JAKEY: I knew there was somethin. Sorry.

KERRIE: Oh Jakey, yer'll have to go back.

JAKEY: Come on I'm knackered.

KERRIE: I want this to be just right for when she gets here.

JAKEY: I know but I need a shower.

KERRIE: I've made a menu now.

KERRIE picks up a homemade menu from the table and shows it JAKEY.

KERRIE: *(Reading.)* Dessert: Apple Pie and Custard.

JAKEY: Cross out custard and put jam.

KERRIE: Apple pie and jam?

CAMERON: We haven't got any jam.

JAKEY: Marmalade then.

KERRIE: I want this dinner to be special.

JAKEY: Apple pie and marmalade is special.

KERRIE: I just wanna show her how much we appreciate her.

JAKEY: It's only Auntie Carol.

KERRIE: She's been a big help these last couple of weeks. Yer wouldn't have a job if it wasn't for her.

CAMERON: *(Beat.)* I'll... I'll go.

KERRIE: To the shop?

CAMERON: Yeah.

KERRIE: I can't go with yer.

CAMERON: I know, I'll er... I'll go on me own.

KERRIE: Okay.

JAKEY takes out some money and hands it to CAMERON.

CAMERON: Can I buy Nuts with the change?

JAKEY: Yeah but don't get them cashews, they knock me sick.

CAMERON: I mean the magazine.

JAKEY: *(Laughs.)* Yeah, alright.

CAMERON leaves through the front way.

JAKEY: Get on that.

KERRIE: I'm made up for him.

JAKEY: Did yer go to that open day at the college?

KERRIE: Yeah. They said I had to get 5 A-Cs, including English, Maths and Science to do the course.

JAKEY: Any chance of that like?

KERRIE: I don't know, I'm way behind. I'll give it a go though.

JAKEY: First bridge yer build yer can name it after me.

KERRIE: Yeah, okay. One step at/ a

JAKEY's phone goes. He answers it.

JAKEY: Alright. *(Beat.)* What? *(Pause.)* I can't lad. *(Pause.)* I'll see what I can do tomorrow.

JAKEY hangs up.

KERRIE: It's them innit?

JAKEY doesn't answer.

KERRIE: They're never gonna leave yer alone are they?

JAKEY: *(Beat.)* There's smoke comin out the oven!

KERRIE: What???

KERRIE spins round.

JAKEY: Got yer!

She grabs a handful of blackberries from a bowl near the cooker and chases JAKEY out of the door.

KERRIE: Come here!!!

JAKEY: Where's yer sense of humour girl?

End.

OTHER LAURENCE WILSON TITLES

Lost Monsters
£8.99 / 9781840029291

Urban Legend
£7.99 / 9781840024906

WWW.OBERONBOOKS.COM

Follow us on www.twitter.com/@oberonbooks
& www.facebook.com/oberonbook